Computer English

Martin Eayrs

Penguin Quick Guides Series Editors:
Andy Hopkins and Jocelyn Potter

PENGUIN ENGLISH

Pearson Education Limited
Edinburgh Gate
Harlow
Essex CM20 2JE, England
and Associated Companies throughout the world.

ISBN 0 582 46886 8

First published 2001
Text copyright © Martin Eayrs 2001

The moral right of the author has been asserted.

Produced for the publisher by Bluestone Press, Charlbury, UK.
Designed and typeset by White Horse Graphics, Charlbury, UK.
Illustrations by Roger Fereday (Linda Rogers Associates).
Photography by Patrick Ellis.
Printed and bound in Denmark by Norhaven A/S, Viborg.

Published by Pearson Education Limited in association with
Penguin Books Ltd, both companies being subsidiaries of Pearson plc.

For a complete list of the titles available from Penguin English visit
our website at www.penguinenglish.com, or please write to your local
Pearson Education office or to: Marketing Department, Penguin Longman
Publishing, 5 Bentinck Street, London W1U 2EG.

Contents

Getting started

How can this book help you?

Do you want to read and talk about computers in English? Perhaps you know *what* you want to say … but not *how*, because you don't know the right words? *The Penguin Quick Guide to Computer English* can help you find the words that you're looking for.

What's in this book?

Each chapter looks at different areas relating to computers – things like hardware, word processing and the Internet. At the end of every chapter you'll find exercises to help you remember what you've learned. The book starts with buying and setting up basic equipment, goes through various uses of computers – at work, in education, looks at games and the

Internet, and finishes off with a look at the future. All the words in the book are also listed in the **Index**, where there is space to write them in your own language.

Why is this book called a *Quick Guide*?

- Because it's short and takes you straight to the words you need. What's more, it's small enough to carry around with you.

- Because it gives you a small amount of language that you really need to know, it is also quick to learn.

How do I use the book?

- Either read the book from start to finish or select a relevant chapter. For example, you may want to go straight to the chapter called

Fun and games, which presents useful language for using computers for recreational purposes.

- Do the exercises in the **Review** at the end of the chapter. Then go to the **Answers** section at the back. Were you right?

- Try out the language as soon as you get a chance.

I hope you enjoy using the book and that you find it useful.

Mouse to
modem

1

Buying the basics

Well, there's the HD5079Q ... or the 764PP ... or of course, the LLT0127 ...

FOR SALE

Used PC with 15" **monitor,
mouse, keyboard** and all
cables, £250 o.n.o. Very
good condition.

I also have a 56k **modem**
(for the Internet) and a
scanner (to copy pictures)
if you are interested.

Phone Angela
on 638290, evenings.

monitor

mouse

keyboard

modem

scanner

Printers

John: What **printer** should I buy?

Alex: Well, **dot matrix** printers are fast and cheap but the **output** doesn't look very clear. If you want high quality output you need a **laser** or **ink jet** printer.

John: Can they print in colour?

Alex: Yes, but colour laser printers are very expensive. Ink jet printers can print high quality colour and are much cheaper than laser printers.

printer

dot matrix

output

laser

ink jet

Disk drives

And I use that one to hold my coffee.

Alex: I've just bought these **disks** to **back up** my files in case my computer **crashes**.

Paul: Good idea. I bought a Zip **drive** last year because my files were too large to **save** to disk. Now the Zip disks are too small for my backups!

Alex: What are you going to do?

Paul: I think I'll buy a CD drive and **burn** the files on to rewritable CDs.

disk

back up

crash

drive

save

burn

Portable computers

You can work anywhere these days.

A **palmtop** is small enough to fit in your pocket and lets you carry all your vital information around with you.

A **laptop** has all the advantages of a **desktop** computer but is more **portable** and runs off batteries. With a **mobile phone** you can have immediate access to the Internet.

palmtop

laptop

desktop

portable

mobile phone

Almost ready

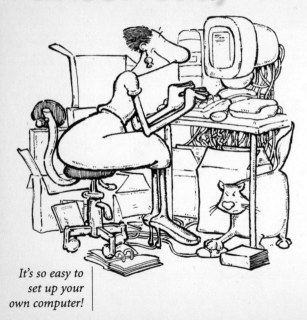

It's so easy to set up your own computer!

Computer manual

a) After you have connected the **hardware** (computer, monitor, keyboard, mouse, printer, etc.), you will need to **install** the system **software** on to your hard disk from a system disk or CD.

b) You will then need to **restart** and your computer should **boot** automatically from the hard disk.

c) When the operating system is successfully installed, you can install your computer **programs** and other software.

hardware

install

software

restart

boot

program *(n)*

Review 1

A Complete the sentences with these words.

burn   output   backups   installed   portable

1 Make .... of files in case your computer crashes.
2 You can .... files on to a CD.
3 System software is often .... on new computers.
4 A .... computer is useful when travelling.
5 Laser printers provide good quality .....

B Match 1–4 with a–d.

1 hardware
2 modem
3 crash
4 laptop

a) a portable computer
b) if this happens you have to reboot
c) the physical parts of a computer
d) it lets you communicate over the telephone system

The computer invasion

2

They're taking over

The new
pet
passport.

Everywhere we go we use computer technology to **process** information.

Supermarkets read the **bar code** on the food you buy with **laser scanners**.

Pay phones and **ATMs*** can read the information on a phone or credit card with **magnetic strip readers** and some can even record information onto the card.

process

bar code

laser scanner

ATM

magnetic strip reader

*Automated Teller Machines

Invasion at home

All this technology and I get a power cut.

A recent Government report says that the number of household appliances containing **microprocessors** has doubled in the last five years.

Although twenty years ago video machines and radio-cassette recorders could record when the owner was away, today's washing machines, microwaves and fridges can all be **programmed** with the owner's instructions.

The change has hit children's toys and games too. Many of today's toys and games contain **silicon chips** and have **LEDs*** and **screens** that can display text and **graphics**.

micro-processor

program *(v)*

silicon chip

LED

screen

graphics

*Light-Emitting Diodes

In the car

Dad, this TV show is really boring …

Get a CarPC computer in your car

- Never get lost again with our **GPS*** navigation system

- Monitor your engine's performance

- Entertain your passengers with games, CDs, DVDs, MP3s, TV and radio

- Full access to **Internet** and **e-mail**, fax and **pager** messages

- The **liquid crystal** display and infrared keyboard fit into the dashboard and the microprocessor unit can be safely installed in the boot.

GPS

Internet

e-mail

pager

liquid crystal

*Global Positioning System

Don't be disadvantaged

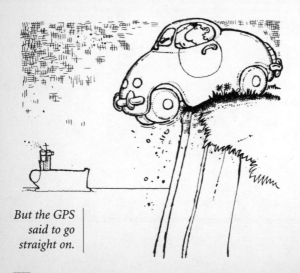

But the GPS said to go straight on.

Helping people with difficulties

- GPS is useful if you have difficulty seeing – our **satellites** work out where you are and where you want to go.
- **Voice recognition** software – you speak and your computer types or responds to your instructions.
- **Voice synthesizers** – you type and your computer speaks for you.
- **Remote controlled** systems – software to control your wheelchair.

  For more information: www.technoUwant.com

satellite

voice recognition

voice synthesizer

remote control

Inputting
information

Look after your mouse.

Ask Nick the Nerd

Nick the Nerd answers readers' questions

Q: How do text and pictures get into a computer?

A: Text and **images** can be **copied** from another disk or **downloaded** from the Internet. Text can be typed in or scanned and then converted to text using **OCR***.

Images can also be scanned or drawn directly on the screen. This can be done with a mouse and **mouse pad** but a stylus and **digitizing tablet** will give better control.

image

copy

download

OCR

mouse
pad

digitizing
tablet

* Optical Character Recognition

Review 2

A Use these words to complete the sentences.

screen digitizing synthesizer recognition
bar codes Positioning

1 The letters GPS stand for Global .... System.
2 Laser scanners read .... in supermarkets.
3 A computer .... can display text and graphics.
4 Voice .... software converts speech into text.
5 A voice .... can convert printed text into words.
6 Graphic artists draw with a stylus and .... tablet.

B Match 1–4 with a–d.

1 chip	a) You do this to get files from the
2 liquid	Internet.
3 satellite	b) Car computers know their
4 download	position from .... information.
	c) Some monitor screens have ....
	crystal displays.
	d) The heart of a computer is a
	silicon .....

Working with computers

3

Online banking

Now where am I supposed to put this?

EAGLE BANK

Welcome to Eagle
online banking.

Enter your **user ID** and
password and **click** on the
log on button.

*User ID: ....

*Password: ....

[**Log On**]   [**Help**]

* Your user ID is the number you received
with your reference pack. Your password is
the word you chose when you filled out the
application form.

enter

user ID

password

click

log on

Doctors at work

Yes, there's a nasty bug going around …

WIVENHOME MEDICAL
SERVICE

IT SUPPORT OFFICER

Applications are invited from **IT*** qualified graduates with experience of working in a medical environment. The position involves management of **telemedicine** services, maintenance of medical **databases** and internal **bulletin board** and supervision of **monitoring systems** throughout the hospital. Excellent salary package.

See <u>WMS home page</u> for more details.

IT

telemedicine

database

bulletin board

monitoring system

* Information Technology

39

First day

WORKSTATION 25 • Ms TRACEY POTTER

Why do they call these workstations?

MEMO

To:	Tracey Potter
From:	Frank Malpas
Date:	25 March, 2001

You'll be at **workstation** number 25 this week. For user ID in Eagle we use the initial letter of someone's first name **dot** the first three letters of their surname; in your case, 'T.Pot'. It'll also be your e-mail ID. When you log on for the first time use SESAME as your password – you can change it to whatever you like afterwards. You can **access** the whole office **network** from your **terminal**.

workstation

dot

access

network

terminal

All change

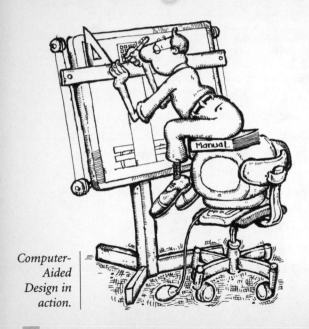

Computer-Aided Design in action.

60 Years at Eagle

I can remember when we didn't have any computers in this factory. Now they are everywhere. **Spreadsheet** and **EFT*** programs in the Finance Departments; Graphics and **CAD**** software in the Research and Design departments; **teleconferencing** with our Tokyo and Caracas offices; databases to store our records and organise our mailings; and of course absolutely everybody has a **word processor**.

spreadsheet

EFT

CAD

tele-
conferencing

word
processor

*Electronic Funds Transfer
**Computer-Aided Design

Book production

The designer selected the fonts.

To produce this book the text was first typed and then **imported** from a word processor and into a DTP* program. Then the designer selected the **fonts** – that's the style for the text. The cartoons were drawn by hand and scanned into the DTP **application** as graphics **files**.

import

font

application

file

*Desktop Publishing

Review 3

A Complete the sentences with words from this chapter.

1 You can use .... software for financial calculations.

2 .... software stores and manipulates data.

3 For writing letters we use a .....

4 Architects use .... software to design buildings.

B Match 1–4 with a–d.

1 application   a) I .... to my computer in
2 log on   the morning.
3 enter   b) I .... my ID number and
4 access   password.
                 c) Then I can .... all the files on
                   the network.
                 d) A type of program.

Education

4

Ordering equipment

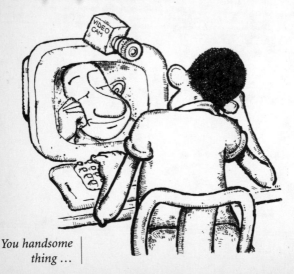

You handsome thing …

Dear Headteacher

Re: Request for additional computer equipment

You asked me to give you some suggestions for additional computer equipment for next year.

The computers in the music department need to have **soundcards** installed so that they can play music. We need a **videocam** so that we can put live pictures of the school onto the Internet. We need a new **server** to manage all our computers because the one we have is too slow. We need new **hard disks** because we need more memory. Finally we need more educational software (on **CD-ROMs**) for the library.

soundcard

videocam

server

hard disk

CD-ROM

Homework

I'm in the condor chat room.

Mother: You're supposed to be doing your homework!

Child: Oh, Mum. This is my homework. I have to **search** on the **Web** for information about condors.

Mother: But what's all that noise?

Child: Oh, that? I'm in the condor **chat room**. I'm talking to someone in Argentina.

Mother: There's a condor chat group?

Child: Yes, look. I joined the condor **e-list** as well … I got twenty-three **mails*** already today.

search

Web

chat room

e-list

mail

* mails = e-mails = messages

Computer lab

St Hilda's **Computer Lab**

Winter Term –
LANGUAGE TRAINING SKILLS 1

Session 7 (Word processing skills) will be held today at 17.00. We shall be looking at using **spell checkers** and online dictionaries.

Timetables for sessions 8 (Using **grammar and style checkers**), 9 (The basics of **hypertext**) and 10 (Introduction to **interactive exercises***) will be given out during session 7.

(*No programming skills required – creating online responses to interactive exercises will be covered in session 27)

Please contact the Help Desk for further information.

computer lab

spell checker

grammar and style checker

hypertext

interactive exercise

Learning alone

Sometimes CAL
is not enough.

Computer Assisted Learning (CAL) techniques can provide many activities for learners.

Some examples:

- **Authoring** software allows teachers to assemble different kinds of exercises with their own materials.

- **Computer adaptive tests** give students fast and accurate indications of their ability.

- **Programmed learning** routines allow students to learn at their own speed.

- **Computer simulations** allow students to experience potentially dangerous situations safely.

Computer Assisted Learning

authoring

computer adaptive test

programmed learning

computer simulation

Words ...

FLAMBOROUGH
UNIVERSITY

English Language Department

THE FLAMBOROUGH
ENGLISH LANGUAGE CORPUS
Over the last five years the
University has assembled a **corpus**
of over 10 million words of English
text. This large body of **e-text** is
available for online consultation by
students registered on onsite and
distance learning courses. Contact
the English Language department
for further information or join the
departmental **discussion group**.

corpus

e-text

distance learning

discussion group

Review 4

A Complete these with words from this chapter.

1 To discuss a special topic join a .... group.
2 A computer lab usually has one .... and many workstations.
3 You can send pictures across the Internet if you have a .....
4 You need a .... if you want to hear music.
5 In a .... group you can communicate immediately with people all over the world.

B Match 1–4 with a–d.

1 hard
2 simulations
3 corpus
4 chat group

a) A large number of electronic texts.
b) A real-time discussion group.
c) Pilots learn to fly by using .....
d) Keep your files on the .... disk.

Fun
and
games

5

Games console

And they say young people have no concentration nowadays …

The ultimate video gaming experience

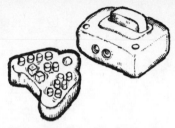

The Xema 67/A games **console** revolutionizes gameplay. Comes with de luxe 14 **button** remote control **gamepad** and connecting cable. Simply **load** any of our exceptional Xemgame **cartridges** and connect to TV or monitor for instant fun.

Cat. No. 364/4732

£27.50

console

button

gamepad

load

cartridge

Games

That computer's got more memory than you.

Well, for games you're looking at one of our **multimedia** computers. It needs to be able to handle **multitasking** – that's doing a number of tasks at the same time. There's the Delphi 574 model for £720 – with sound and **graphics cards**. It's got 64 megabyte of RAM and you can buy some extra **memory**. I'll give you a few games as well and I'll include a **joystick** for free …

multimedia

multi-tasking

graphics card

memory

joystick

More games

Can Johnny come out to play?

ANNUAL REPORT

Prestwick Software

■ Games division

Total sales for computer games have remained stable over the year. The fall in sales of our classic **text adventure games** has been matched by increased revenue from **arcade games**, particularly **shoot-'em-ups**. Sales for **strategy games** dipped in the last quarter, while figures for **board games** (including card games) have been consistent. Our planned move into online gaming remains on target.

text adventure game

arcade game

shoot-'em-up

strategy game

board game

On holiday

A: Enjoying your holiday ?

B: You bet! Where are you going?

A: To the **cybercafe** to **check** my e-mail. Then I thought I'd pick up a couple of **DVDs** to watch on my laptop tonight.

B: I'll come with you. I can download some **MP3s** while I'm waiting. Or maybe just **surf** the Web a bit – see what I can find …

A: Cool! Let's go.

cybercafe

check

DVD

MP3

surf

Pictures

They've cropped that picture badly.

Ask Nick the Nerd

Q: What's the difference between **bitmap** and **vector** images?

A: Vector images are drawn according to a mathematical formula and look the same at any size. When you work with vector images you work with the whole image as an object.

Bitmap images are made up of **pixels** (picture elements) and you can change the colour of each individual pixel. Bitmap images are distorted if you change the size.

Both kinds of image can be **cropped**, making any or all of the edges of the image disappear.

bitmap

vector

pixel

crop

Review 5

A Complete these with words from this chapter.

1 A .... image is made up of individual pixels.
2 Music is often saved in .... files.
3 You can go to a .... to check your e-mail.
4 To view a picture at any size you should save the file as a .... image.
5 Games for a console are usually bought on .....
6 When I have time on my hands I like to .... the Web to see what I can find.

B Match 1–3 with a–c.

1 DVD   a) To cut part of a picture.
2 joystick   b) You need this for some games.
3 crop   c) Movies are available in this format.

Speaking to the world

6

Web search

*He's got the
biggest
website I've
ever seen!*

To find us here at Penguin if you don't know the web address ...

- Log on to the Internet.

- Open your **browser** and type in the address of a **search engine**.

- In the search engine window type the words *Penguin English*.

- Click on the **link** to the main Penguin site and then **navigate** to the page you want.

- When you find it, **bookmark** it so you can find it again.

And that's it – easy, isn't it?

browser

search engine

link

navigate

bookmark

Website

I'm the master of this web and don't you forget it ...

MAGNET
ISP

Thinking of setting up your own **website**? Want to be your own **webmaster**? It's easier than you think.

Let us register your **domain** for you (*.com*, *.org* and *.co.uk* are all available). Get your site up quickly with our easy-to-use web tools kit.

And soon you can be looking at your own **home page** instead of ours.

Magnet – the **ISP*** people stick to.

Contact us at …

website

webmaster

domain

home page

ISP

* Internet Service Provider

Moving files

Ask Nick the Nerd

Q: What is a **static IP**?

A: A static IP (Internet Protocol) number gives a computer a unique address and identity on the Internet. If you connect to the Internet by modem, each time you log on you use the same IP number.

Some service providers require you to have a static IP number in order to use **FTP** (File Transfer Protocol) software for **uploading** and downloading files. And remember you will have to set and acquire access **privileges** to be able to log on to one machine from another.

static IP

FTP

upload

privilege

Electronic lists

Be courteous – don't flame others.

From: "Michael Jones"
<m.jones@alpha.centauri.com>
To: <administrator_Condor-L@thu.edu>
Subject: Re: List rules
Date: Thu, 17 Aug 2000 07:16:36 +0200
X-Priority: 3

Welcome to the Condor-L discussion list.
The rules are very simple.

- **Post** messages to
  <Condor-L@thu.edu>.
- No insults (**flaming**) or mass-mailing
  of irrelevant material (**spamming**).
- If your mail is **bounced** back to us as
  'undeliverable' three times we will take
  you off the list.
- **Lurkers** (people who read messages
  and don't post) are welcome – but
  remember you can post too!
- For Help contact me at
  <M.Jones@thu.edu>.

Michael Jones
mailto: Condor-L@thu.edu .

post

flame

spam

bounce

lurker

Netiquette

Netiquette is all about good manners.

Basic **netiquette** (good manners)
for the **newbie** (or newcomer)

- Always read the **FAQ*** file first if
  you have a question
- Don't spam others with stuff they
  don't want
- Be courteous – don't flame others
- Edit out unnecessary text when
  you reply to mails
- Don't **SHOUT** – capital letters
  are offensive and hard to read
- Do not forward mails without
  permission of sender
- Don't criticise other people's
  grammar or spelling
- Keep your **signature** short and
  relevant

netiquette

newbie

FAQ

shout

signature

* Frequently Asked Questions

Review 6

A Complete these with words from this chapter.

1 Using capitals in e-mails is called .....
2 A .... is a beginner in e-mail and chat groups.
3 To return to a web page easily you can .... it.
4 A .... is a program for surfing the web.
5 If an e-mail message is .... it is returned undelivered to the sender.

B Match 1–4 with a–d.

1 ISP a) Politeness on the Internet.
2 domain b) E-mails you don't want.
3 netiquette c) A company that provides
4 spam   Internet access.
           d) Most companies register
              an Internet .....

Programs

7

Problems

My screen keeps on freezing …

A: Hello, Grapefruit technical support. How can I help?

B: Hi. I've got a problem with the display on my monitor. Whenever I move my **cursor** out of the active **window** the cursor disappears.

A: Mmm. Anything else unusual?

B: Yes. Some of the **menu** options keep disappearing and sometimes when I double click on the hard disk **icon** the screen **freezes**.

A: Sounds like a software problem to me. Have you tried …

cursor

window

menu

icon

freeze

Managing files

Moving files is simply a drag …

FILE ORGANISATION

You can organise your files in **directories**, sometimes called **folders**. To create a folder go to the Desktop File Menu and choose 'New Directory' or 'New Folder'. Give the directory or folder a name and press **Return**.

To move files between directories **select** the file icon and **drag** it into an open directory or on to the icon of the directory if it is closed.

directory

folder

return

select

drag

Menu options

EDITING A TEXT –
USEFUL COMMANDS

HELP

UNDO	Takes you back to before the last command you performed.
FORMAT	Opens menu with text, paragraph and style options.
DELETE	Removes selected text or objects.
SORT	Sorts selected text in ascending or descending alphanumerical order.
FIND	Finds word or groups of words in selected text.
REPLACE	Replaces text and styles with new ones.

undo

format

delete

sort

replace

Program development

I think that must have been a beta version.

PRESS RELEASE

ASTRAL 9.0 BETA VERSION

Galaxy Software is pleased to announce the latest public **beta version*** of its market leader astrology software, Astral 9.0b.

Registered users of Astral 8.X will be eligible for free **upgrades** to version 9.0 when it is released as a **full version**. Users of other earlier versions of Astral should visit our web site for details of free **updates** and upgrade options.

Our bottom line product Astral Lite will continue to be available as **freeware**.

beta version

upgrade

full version

update

freeware

*Beta version software is still in final testing stage and may contain bugs and minor problems.

Writing software

The trouble is we just aren't speaking the same language …

FAQs – Computer Languages

Computer languages range from the incomprehensible – pure **machine languages**, expressed directly in **binary** code and consisting of long strings of 0s and 1s – through **assembly languages** – to the **high-level languages** (HLLs) used by human programmers, such as C+++ or Java.

Assembly languages make programs written in high-level languages smaller and faster by ensuring that each statement corresponds to one of a set of binary instructions that the **CPU*** recognises.

machine language

binary

assembly language

high-level language

CPU

*Central Processing Unit

Review 7

A Complete these with words from this chapter.

1 Pre-release software is tested in a .... version.
2 .... code consists of a series of 1s and 0s.
3 If your cursor ...., restart the computer.
4 Folders are places to keep all your .... tidy.

B Match 1–4 with a–d.

1 undo
2 CPU
3 freeware
4 cursor

a) Free software.
b) This moves on the screen when you move the mouse.
c) This controls computer operations.
d) If you make a mistake you can usually .... it.

Mbd· contempl shur

%$PLAपp°ăp

vST icicity467

Text
and
numbers

8

Text

Why are you painting a portrait in a landscape format?

Create eye-catching documents easily with our new budget word processing program, Textfine.

With Textfine you can:

- work in **portrait** or **landscape** format

- **customize** page sizes – make pages as large or small as you like

- **scroll** the visible screen horizontally and vertically

- **cut and paste** text and graphics between different Textfine documents

- store items on Textfine's **clipboard**

- import text or graphics from other applications

portrait

landscape

customize

scroll

cut and paste

clipboard

Formatting

Here are two lines of
left **aligned** text

Here are two lines of
right aligned text

Here are two lines of
centred text

This paragraph has been **justified** (see the level margins on both sides) – and also contains **bold**, *italic*, ***bold italic***, <u>underlined</u> and ~~strike through~~ characters.

aligned

centred

justified

bold

italic

strike through

Adding interest

Use bullets to make your point clear.

There are many ways to make a text look more interesting. Some people sometimes like to start a paragraph with a **drop cap** (as at the beginning of this paragraph).

Other things you can do include:

● using **bullets** to make points stand out

using different fonts and type styles

    using **tabs** to **indent** your text

By careful use of these tools you can create clear and stylish documents.

drop cap

bullet

tab

indent

Text tools

Clip art …

Additional features in Textfine:

- an extensive library of **clip art** livens up your texts

- a dictionary, grammar and style checker to improve your writing

- a **thesaurus** helps you find the right word

- **style sheets** allow you to change document styles easily

- **mail merge** lets you integrate your address book with your mail

- an onscreen **word count** counts your words while you type

- **wizards** help you set up different types of document

clip art

thesaurus

style
sheet

mail
merge

word
count

wizard

Numbers

Typing text in a cell.

A: How's that spreadsheet coming along?

B: Don't ask! I've got a problem with a **formula** in one of the **cells**!

A: Let's have a look. Yes, here, look – you've left a bracket unclosed.

B: Thanks. I'll just set the **word wrap** on the text cells and I can print it out. Do you want the data displayed as a **pie chart** or a **bar graph**?

A: A pie chart will be fine.

formula

cell

word wrap

pie chart

bar graph

Review 8

A Complete these with words from this chapter.

1 Drag and .... is one way of transferring files from one folder to another.

2 You can copy text from one document to another using the .... and paste commands.

3 If you want to add simple images to a text document you can import .... art.

4 You can use .... or italic text to make a word stand out in a sentence.

5 You can show the relative proportions of mathematical data by using a .... chart.

6 If a page is displayed horizontally it is referred to as .... layout.

Security

9

System failure

You may have a software bug.

WHEN ALL ELSE FAILS

If your computer **hangs**, freezes or you experience **system failure**:

- Restart the computer and run a disk repair **utility** to examine the disk and files for structural damage.

- Reinstall system software.

- If the problem continues, you may have a software **bug**. Try removing and reinstalling applications one at a time.

- Back up all essential files, reformat the disk and reinstall the software.

hang

system failure

utility

bug

Sabotage

And when we get in there we'll go for the system files.

Ask Nick the Nerd

Q: What's the difference between a **Trojan horse**, a **worm** and a **virus**?

A: Trojan horses are programs that seem to do something useful or entertaining but can cause damage. Worms are self-replicating programs that live in active memory and are usually not noticed until system resources slow down or stop.

Viruses infect program files. If an infected file is passed to another machine the virus goes with it. **Attachments** and word processor documents containing **macros** can also carry viruses.

Trojan horse

worm

virus

attachment

macro

Hacking

*Him?
Oh, he's a
Christmas
cracker …*

Ask Nick the Nerd

Q: What's the difference between **hackers**, **crackers** and **phreakers**?

A: Hackers love to explore computers and computer systems for their own sake. Some but not all are **nerds**. Most hackers are not criminals.

Crackers try to break security on computer systems – getting through **firewalls** and password systems, and are looked down on by many hackers as being dishonest and technically inferior.

Phreakers are basically interested in cracking telephone systems, once as a challenge, often nowadays for financial gain.

hacker

cracker

phreaker

nerd

firewall

Protection

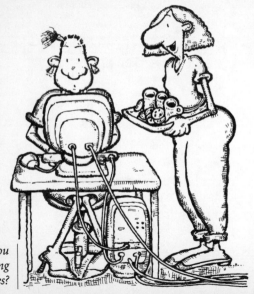

Are you accepting cookies?

HOW SAFE IS YOUR COMPUTER?

Unless you are an expert, you may not know. But don't worry, we do – it's our business.

Let us tell you about:

- Data **encryption** and **decryption** software that prevents anyone reading your files without your permission
- **Secure server** facilities for online transactions
- The truth about the **cookies** that web sites leave in your computer
- How to get your own **digital signature**

Phone today on 043-8109 for free advice. And you'll never have to worry again.

encryption

decryption

secure server

cookie

digital signature

Is it legal?

Software pirates.

Exclusive independent school White Cliffs College is today facing a £400,000 fine for failure to produce **site licenses** for software on its computer networks.

The case came to light when sixth-formers at the school were discovered trying to sell proprietary software in an IRC **Warez** channel commonly used for trading **shareware** and other commercially produced programmes. Material supplied by the students is said to have contained digital **watermarks** which clearly indicated that it was **pirated software**.

site license

Warez

shareware

watermark

pirated software

Review 9

Complete these with words from this chapter.

1 E-mail .... can contain macro viruses.
2 If you use multiple copies of a piece of software you need a .... license.
3 The police raided the office looking for .... software.
4 Antiobotix is a .... protection program.
5 Many files have an invisible .... which can track their distribution.
6 Many servers protect their users with a .... that can not be entered without an authenticated password.
7 A software bug can cause your computer to .....

Present and future

10

State of the art

Voice recognition software was becoming more common.

By the beginning of the 21st century, twin CPU computers had made **parallel processing** standard in the personal computer market. Voice recognition and **touch screen** technology was becoming more accessible although screen **resolution** was in most cases still limited to 1024 x 738 and limited **bandwidth** between ISP and consumer did not yet permit full live video transmission.

The most exciting innovation as the century dawned was the implementation of **Bluetooth** technology that would allow users to communicate between all their computer and telephone equipment without the need for cables.

parallel processing

touch screen

resolution

bandwidth

Bluetooth

MP3 revolution

Improved file compression techniques were welcomed.

As more and more **infotainment** and **edutainment** networks emerged, the traditional divisions between computers, video, TV and telephone services rapidly blurred.

Improved file **compression** techniques and increased bandwidth also led to more and more pirated MP3 and MIDI **synthesizer** audio files on the net. Users quickly learned to **rip** files off CDs and convert them to the much smaller MP3 files, burning them onto CDs or uploading them to web sites where anyone could download them.

infotainment

edutainment

compression

synthesizer

rip

Future trends

In the future we'll be able to choose between **wearable computers** and smaller and lighter portables with greater memory than we can imagine today.

We'll use **digital cash** for most things we buy, with electronic **smart cards** that can be recharged with credit at any convenient terminal.

With **network computers** we'll be able to work at any computer, anywhere, and with better **plug and play** between different types of computer, technology hardware incompatibility will be a thing of the past.

wearable computer

digital cash

smart card

network computer

plug and play

Future technology

MEMO

To:	Nick Hodges
From:	Debbie Arnold
Date:	19 September, 2003

1. You asked about **biometric** ID systems. We can certainly install palm print recognition software to control access to the building.
2. I note your comments on the **animated** company logo and have asked our **web publishing** division to replace it on all company correspondence.
3. I have tried to make the terminal **interface** in the reception more **user-friendly** as requested.

Debbie

biometric

animated

web publishing

interface

user-friendly

Close encounters

They're asking for tonight's lottery results.

London, 2004: First contact with Alpha Centauri

As the world reels over news of contact with the aliens transmitting from the region of Alpha Centauri, scientists are working round the clock on deciphering the content of these 'messages'.

Using techniques learned through research into **artificial intelligence** and **machine translation** the world's largest **number crunchers** are working full time on the problem.

One difficulty is the sheer volume of data, flooding in on parallel receivers with combined **real time** speeds of over 200 **gigabytes** a second, faster than …

artificial intelligence

machine translation

number cruncher

real time

gigabyte

Review 10

Complete these with words from this chapter.

1 A .... is bigger than a megabyte.
2 With .... and play technology there is no need to restart equipment or install software.
3 With broader ...., data can be transmitted faster.
4 A monitor's .... determines the quality of the screen image.
5 An .... graphic can give the impression of a moving image.
6 Audio files can be .... from a CD and saved as MP3 files.
7 In the future .... will be used instead of real paper money.
8 Language problems will slowly disappear as .... programs improve.

Index

Your language

access /ækses/
You can access the files with a password. _____

aligned /əlaɪnd/
The text is aligned on the left. _____

animated /ænɪmeɪtəd/
A lot of web pages have animated text. _____

application /æplɪkeɪʃən/
Applications perform specific tasks. _____

arcade game /ɑːkeɪd ɡeɪm/
Seats move in some arcade games. _____

artificial intelligence /ɑːtɪfɪʃəl ɪntelɪdʒəns/
*Research into artificial intelligence is
essential for the future of robotics.* _____

assembly language /əsembli læŋɡwɪdʒ/
*Assembly language is translated into
machine code by assemblers.* _____

ATM /eɪ tiː em/
You can get money from an ATM. _____

attachment /ətætʃmənt/
E-mail attachments can carry viruses. _____

Your language

authoring /ɔːθərɪŋ/
Teachers can use authoring software. _____

back up /bæk ʌp/
Back up your files on a Zip disk. _____

bandwidth /bændwɪdθ/
Broader bandwidth speeds transmission. _____

bar code /bɑː kəʊd/
We've got bar code readers in our shop. _____

bar graph /bɑː grɑːf/
Present your data in a bar graph. _____

beta version /biːtə vɜːʃən/
This is the beta version! _____

binary /baɪnəri/
Most files are text files or binary files. _____

biometric /baɪəʊmetrɪk/
It is a biometric security device. _____

bitmap /bɪtmæp/
A bitmap is a kind of image. _____

Bluetooth /bluːtuːθ/
Bluetooth technology is very new. _____

Your language

board game /bɔːd geɪm/
It's a board game for computers. _____

bold /bəʊld/
Bold text helps words to stand out. _____

bookmark /bʊkmɑːk/
I bookmarked the website for later. _____

boot /buːt/
The computer will boot automatically. _____

bounce /baʊns/
My mails to you keep bouncing. _____

browser /braʊzə/
A browser allows you to access the Web. _____

bug /bʌg/
Bugs can make computers act strangely. _____

bulletin board /bʊlətɪn bɔːd/
Bulletin boards are very popular. _____

bullet /bʊlət/
Use bullets for unnumbered lists. _____

burn /bɜːn/
You can burn files on to a CD. _____

Your language

button /bʌtən/
Gamepad buttons control movement. _____

CAD /kæd/
Use CAD software for 3-D design. _____

cartridge /kɑːtrɪdʒ/
Put the game cartridge in the console. _____

CD-ROM /siː diː rɒm/
A CD-ROM holds 680 megabytes. _____

cell /sel/
Cells can hold text, data or formulas. _____

centred /sentəd/
That text is centred. _____

chat room /tʃæt ruːm/
Never give your address in a chat room. _____

check /tʃek/
I'll check my e-mail before we leave. _____

click /klɪk/
Click on the mouse to close the window. _____

clip art /klɪp ɑːt/
The CD has a library of clip art. _____

Your language

clipboard /klɪpbɔːd/
Store the text on the clipboard. _____

compression /kəmpreʃən/
MP3 compression is used for music files. _____

computer adaptive test
/kəmpjuːtər ədæptɪv test/
*Computer adaptive tests can test
language ability quickly.* _____

Computer Assisted Learning
/kəmpjuːtər əsɪstəd lɜːnɪŋ/
*Computer Assisted Learning techniques
are important in education.* _____

computer lab /kəmpjuːtə læb/
Schools nowadays have computer labs. _____

computer simulation
/kəmpjuːtə sɪmjʊleɪʃən/
*Computer simulations provide a safe
learning environment.* _____

console /kɒnsəʊl/
XEMA consoles are tested thoroughly. _____

Your language

cookie /kʊki/
I delete cookies after visiting a web site. _____

copy /kɒpi/
Copying software can be illegal. _____

corpus /kɔːpəs/
A corpus is a database of language. _____

CPU /siː piː juː/
The CPU is the heart of the computer. _____

cracker /krækə/
He's a cracker. _____

crash /kræʃ/
Oh no! My computer's crashed. _____

crop /krɒp/
Crop the picture – take the top off. _____

cursor /kɜːsə/
Move the cursor with the mouse. _____

customize /kʌstəmaɪz/
Can I customize the page size? _____

cut and paste /kʌt ən peɪst/
Cut and paste text between documents. _____

Your language

cybercafe /saɪbəkæfeɪ/
Cybercafes are very useful for travellers. _____

database /deɪtəbeɪs/
A database stores information. _____

decryption /diːkrɪpʃən/
You need decryption software. _____

delete /dɪliːt/
I've deleted those files. _____

desktop /desktɒp/
I use a desktop computer at home. _____

digital cash /dɪdʒɪtəl kæʃ/
Buy on the Internet with digital cash. _____

digital signature /dɪdʒɪtəl sɪgnətʃə/
Digital signatures authenticate EFTs. _____

digitizing tablet /dɪdʒɪtaɪzɪŋ tæblət/
A digitizing tablet helps you draw. _____

directory /daɪrektəri/
Directories are for storing files. _____

discussion group /dɪskʌʃən gruːp/
E-mail discussion groups can be fun. _____

Your language

disk /dɪsk/
You can store data on a disk. _____

distance learning /dɪstəns lɜːnɪŋ/
Universities offer distance learning. _____

domain /dəmeɪn/
Domain names often end in .com. _____

dot /dɒt/
We call the site 'eagle dot com'. _____

dot matrix /dɒt meɪtrɪks/
A dot matrix printer is quite cheap. _____

download /daʊnləʊd/
I'll download this web page. _____

drag /dræg/
Drag unwanted files to the bin. _____

drive /draɪv/
There's no disk in the drive. _____

drop cap /drɒp kæp/
Drop caps often start a chapter. _____

DVD /diː viː diː/
DVDs are slowly replacing videos. _____

Your language

edutainment /edjuteɪnmənt/
Edutainment makes learning fun. _____

EFT /iː ef tiː/
EFT transfers funds electronically. _____

e-list /iːlɪst/
I've subscribed to the TESL-L e-list. _____

e-mail /iːmeɪl/
E-mail is a great way to communicate. _____

encryption /enkrɪpʃən/
There are two levels of encryption. _____

enter /entə/
Enter your name and press Return. _____

e-text /iːtekst/
Download e-texts from our web site. _____

FAQ /ef eɪ kjuː/
For information, read the FAQ file. _____

file /faɪl/
Polly saved the files onto a disk. _____

firewall /faɪəwɔːl/
Firewalls protect computer networks. _____

Your language

flame /fleɪm/
He was kicked off the list for flaming. _____

folder /fəʊldə/
Directories are sometimes called folders. _____

font /fɒnt/
Too many fonts together look messy. _____

format /fɔːmæt/
Formatting text makes it more legible. _____

formula /fɔːmjʊlə/
You can put a formula in a cell. _____

freeware /friːweə/
Freeware programs often have viruses. _____

freeze /friːz/
A frozen screen shows no response. _____

FTP /ef tiː piː/
Do you have FTP software? _____

full version /fʊl vɜːʃən/
This is the full version of the software. _____

gamepad /geɪmpæd/
This gamepad has lots of functions. _____

Your language

gigabyte /ˈgɪgəbaɪt/
A gigabyte is 1,024 megabytes. _____

GPS /dʒiː piː es/
GPS tells you where you are. _____

grammar checker /ˈgræmə tʃekə/
Grammar checkers are useful. _____

graphics /ˈgræfɪks/
A monitor displays text and graphics. _____

graphics card /ˈgræfɪks kɑːd/
A graphics card is essential for games. _____

hacker /ˈhækə/
Hackers break into computers. _____

hang /hæŋ/
When I do that, my computer hangs. _____

hard disk /hɑːd dɪsk/
A hard disk stores files and programs. _____

hardware /ˈhɑːdweə/
It's a hardware problem. _____

Your language

high-level language
/haɪ levəl læŋgwɪdʒ/
Java is a high-level language. _____

home page /həʊm peɪdʒ/
There's information on my home page. _____

hypertext /haɪpətekst/
Hypertext let you jump to web pages. _____

icon /aɪkɒn/
An icon is a symbol that represents a file. _____

image /ɪmɪdʒ/
You can save an image as a graphics file. _____

import /ɪmpɔːt/
You can easily import text files. _____

indent /ɪndent/
Indent the first line of a paragraph. _____

infotainment /ɪnfəʊteɪnmənt/
InterTV is a home infotainment system. _____

ink jet /ɪnk dʒet/
My new ink jet printer was under $100. _____

Your language

install /ɪnstɔːl/
New computers have software installed. _____

interactive exercise
/ɪntəræktɪv eksəsaɪz/
*Interactive exercises give immediate
online response.* _____

interface /ɪntəfeɪs/
The interface is really user-friendly. _____

Internet /ɪntənet/
The Internet is the new phone system. _____

ISP /aɪ es piː/
Choose your ISP carefully. _____

IT /aɪ tiː/
IT is taught in schools. _____

italic /ɪtælɪk/
This sentence is typed in italics. _____

joystick /dʒɔɪstɪk/
Many computer games need a joystick. _____

justified /dʒʌstɪfaɪd/
Justified text has straight edges. _____

Your language

keyboard /ki:bɔ:d/
My keyboard has a Euro symbol. _____

landscape /lændskeɪp/
Landscape mode is horizontal. _____

laptop /læptɒp/
You can carry a laptop in a briefcase. _____

laser /leɪzə/
I need a new laser printer. _____

laser scanner /leɪzə skænə/
Laser scanners can read bar codes. _____

LED /el i: di:/
The GX/44 has four red LEDs. _____

link /lɪŋk/
Many old sites have dead links. _____

liquid crystal /lɪkwɪd krɪstəl/
Most laptops have liquid crystal screens. _____

load /ləʊd/
Some programs take for ever to load. _____

log on /lɒg ɒn/
I log on to the network every morning. _____

Your language

lurker /lɜːkə/
80% of e-list subscribers are lurkers. _____

machine language /məʃiːn læŋgwɪdʒ/
Machine language is written in binary. _____

machine translation
/məʃiːn trænsleɪʃən/
Machine translation is still limited. _____

macro /mækrəʊ/
Macros are mini programs. _____

magnetic strip reader
/məgnetɪk strɪp riːdə/
Credit cards can be read with a
magnetic strip reader. _____

mail /meɪl/
I receive hundreds of mails a day. _____

mail merge /meɪl mɜːdʒ/
Mail merge is useful. _____

memory /memərɪ/
Computers need a lot of memory. _____

Your language

menu /menjuː/
Most programs have a menu bar. _____

microprocessor
/maɪkrəʊprəʊsesə/
Everything today has microprocessors. _____

mobile phone /məʊbaɪl fəʊn/
You can get me on my mobile phone. _____

modem /məʊdem/
A dual ISDN modem gives faster access. _____

monitor /mɒnɪtə/
I've got a 17 inch colour monitor. _____

monitoring system
/mɒnɪtərɪŋ sɪstəm/
Many musicians use monitoring systems. _____

mouse /maʊs/
The Macintosh mouse has one button. _____

mouse pad /maʊs pæd/
Use a mouse pad under your mouse. _____

MP3 /em piː θriː/
MP3 files are used for music. _____

Your language

multimedia /mʌltimiːdiə/
I'm giving a multimedia presentation. _____

multitasking /mʌltitɑːskɪŋ/
*Multitasking lets you run more than
one program at once.* _____

navigate /nævɪgeɪt/
Hypertext links help you to navigate. _____

nerd /nɜːd/
He's a strange one – a real nerd. _____

netiquette /netɪket/
Shouting is bad netiquette. _____

network /netwɜːk/
Our company has a huge network. _____

network computer
/netwɜːk kəmpjuːtə/
Network computers need a server. _____

newbie /njuːbɪ/
Newbies are beginners on the Internet. _____

number cruncher /nʌmbə krʌntʃə/
Number crunchers do big calculations. _____

Your language

OCR /əʊ siː ɑː/
OCR converts an image to a text file.

output /aʊtpʊt/
The output isn't high quality.

pager /peɪdʒə/
Pagers let you receive text messages.

palmtop /pɑːmtɒp/
A palmtop is a very small computer.

parallel processing
/pærəlel prəʊsesɪŋ/
*Parallel processing allows computer
programs to work faster.*

password /pæswɜːd/
You need a password to log on.

phreaker /friːkə/
Phreakers make free phone calls.

pie chart /paɪ tʃɑːt/
Pie charts are easy to understand.

pirated software /paɪrətəd sɒftweə/
Pirated software is very common.

Your language

pixel /ˈpɪksəl/
Screen images are made up of pixels. _____

plug and play /ˌplʌg ən ˈpleɪ/
With plug and play devices,
configuration is not necessary. _____

portable /ˈpɔːtəbəl/
Laptops and palmtops are portables. _____

portrait /ˈpɔːtreɪt/
Portrait mode is vertical. _____

post /pəʊst/
Lurkers never post to discussion groups. _____

printer /ˈprɪntə/
Laser printers are getting cheaper. _____

privilege /ˈprɪvəlɪdʒ/
To enter, you need access privileges. _____

process /ˈprəʊses/
A computer processes information. _____

program (n) /ˈprəʊgræm/
Computers must have programs. _____

Your language

program (v) /prəʊgræm/
It's programmed to recognize my voice. _____

programmed learning
/prəʊgræmd lɜːnɪŋ/
*Programmed learning allows different
paths of study.* _____

real time /riːl taɪm/
Real time systems respond immediately. _____

remote control /rɪməʊt kəntrəʊl/
This remote control turns off the TV. _____

replace /rɪpleɪs/
He replaced all the £ signs with $. _____

resolution /rezəluːʃən/
This is a high resolution monitor. _____

restart /riːstɑːt/
Try restarting your computer. _____

return /rɪtɜːn/
Use the Return key to end a paragraph. _____

rip /rɪp/
Just Rippit is for ripping CD tracks. _____

Your language

satellite /ˈsætəlaɪt/
Have you got satellite TV?

save /seɪv/
You should save often while working.

scanner /ˈskænə/
A scanner copies texts and graphics.

screen /skriːn/
I clean my monitor screen every week.

scroll /skrəʊl/
To see the full page, scroll down.

search /sɜːtʃ/
I searched the Web for my name.

search engine /sɜːtʃ endʒɪn/
A search engine searches the Web.

secure server /sɪkjʊə sɜːvə/
Our company has a secure server.

select /sɪlekt/
Double-click on a word to select it.

server /sɜːvə/
We have 10 workstations on this server.

Your language

shareware /ʃeəweə/
Shareware is cheap software. _____

shoot-'em-up /ʃuːt əm ʌp/
Shoot-'em-up games are very popular. _____

shout /ʃaʊt/
To shout in e-lists, use capitals. _____

signature /sɪgnətʃə/
An e-mail signature should be short. _____

silicon chip /sɪlɪkən tʃɪp/
A silicon chip has millions of transistors. _____

site license /saɪt laɪsəns/
A site license is a multi-user license. _____

smart card /smɑːt kɑːd/
Smart cards can be charged at ATMs. _____

software /sɒftweə/
Computers often come with software. _____

sort /sɔːt/
I sorted the text in ascending order. _____

soundcard /saʊndkɑːd/
I need a soundcard to play MP3 files. _____

Your language

synthesizer /sɪnθəsaɪzə/
MIDI is used by most synthesizers. _____

system failure /sɪstəm feɪljə/
Reboot after system failure. _____

tab /tæb/
Adjust columns by changing tab stops. _____

teleconferencing /telikɒnfrənsɪŋ/
Teleconferencing is becoming popular. _____

telemedicine /telimedsɪn/
Telemedicine is online medical help. _____

terminal /tɜːmɪnəl/
There are twelve terminals in the lab. _____

text adventure game
/tekst ədventʃə geɪm/
Text adventure games have no graphics. _____

thesaurus /θəsɔːrəs/
A thesaurus is a dictionary of synonyms. _____

touch screen /tʌtʃ skriːn/
Touch screens make your arms tired. _____

Your language

Trojan horse /trəʊdʒən hɔːs/
Trojan horses cause computer problems. _____

undo /ʌnduː/
Press Ctrl + Z to undo your last action. _____

update /ʌpdeɪt/
This is the latest software update. _____

upgrade /ʌpgreɪd/
I've upgraded to the new version. _____

upload /ʌpləʊd/
I'll upload the files to my web page. _____

user ID /juːzər aɪ diː/
A user ID identifies you on a network. _____

user-friendly /juːzə frendli/
Icons are very user-friendly. _____

utility /juːtɪləti/
Utilities are small programs. _____

vector /vektə/
Scale vector images without quality loss. _____

videocam /vɪdiəʊkæm/
Videocams let you put film on the Web. _____

Your language

virus /vaɪrəs/
Update anti-virus files monthly. _____

voice recognition /vɔɪs rekəgnɪʃən/
Voice recognition software is unreliable. _____

voice synthesizer /vɔɪs sɪnθəsaɪzə/
Voice synthesizers convert text to speech. _____

Warez /weəz/
*'Warez' refers to commercial software
offered for illegal sale.* _____

watermark /wɔːtəmɑːk/
Digital watermarks are invisible. _____

wearable computers
/weərəbəl kəmpjuːtəz/
Wearable computers should be small. _____

Web /web/
The Web is a wonderful place. _____

webmaster /webmɑːstə/
He works as webmaster for two sites. _____

web publishing /web pʌblɪʃɪŋ/
Web publishing uses new technologies. _____

Your language

website /websaɪt/
A website consists of linked pages. _____

window /wɪndəʊ/
I've got 20 windows open on the screen. _____

wizard /wɪzəd/
Wizards help to customize documents. _____

word count /wɜːd kaʊnt/
The word count must be below 2,000. _____

word processor /wɜːd prəʊsesə/
Everyone uses a word processor. _____

word wrap /wɜːd ræp/
Word wrap puts text around objects. _____

workstation /wɜːksteɪʃən/
Workstations are part of a network. _____

worm /wɜːm/
A worm is a virus that replicates itself. _____

Answers

Review 1

A 1 backups 2 burn 3 installed 4 portable 5 output
B 1c 2d 3b 4a

Review 2

A 1 Positioning 2 bar codes 3 screen 4 recognition
  5 synthesizer 6 digitizing
B 1d 2c 3b 4a

Review 3

A 1 spreadsheet 2 Database 3 word processor 4 CAD
B 1d 2a 3c 4b

Review 4

A 1 discussion 2 server 3 videocam 4 soundcard
  5 chat
B 1d 2c 3a 4b

Review 5

A 1 bitmap 2 MP3 3 cybercafe 4 vector
  5 cartridges 6 surf
B 1c 2b 3a

Review 6
A 1 shouting 2 newbie 3 bookmark 4 browser
  5 bounced
B 1c 2d 3a 4b

Review 7
A 1 beta 2 binary 3 freezes 4 files
B 1d 2c 3a 4b

Review 8
A 1 drop 2 cut 3 clip 4 bold 5 pie 6 landscape

Review 9
1 attachments 2 site 3 pirated 4 virus
5 watermark 6 firewall 7 hang

Review 10
1 gigabyte 2 plug 3 bandwidth 4 resolution
5 animated 6 ripped 7 digital cash
8 machine translation